To Jane,

My very special friend

Happy vacation -

I'll miss you

Eil

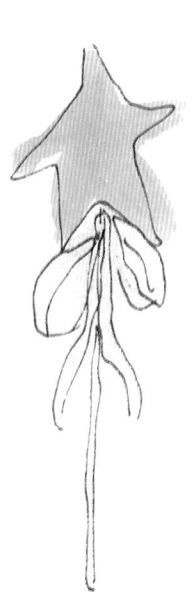

With
Each
Remembrance

A Selection Of
Writings On Memories

By Flavia Weedn

Flavia

APPLAUSE INC.
Woodland Hills, CA 91365-4183
© Flavia Weedn
All Rights Reserved
Special Thanks to All the Flavia Team Members at Applause
Licensed by APPLAUSE Licensing
19894

Library of Congress Catalog Card Number: 89-85003

WITH EACH REMEMBRANCE
Printed in China
ISBN 0-929632-08-7

Remembering is a tool
with which we can
relive moments past.
It lets us see
where we've been and
understand more where we
are going.

Flavia

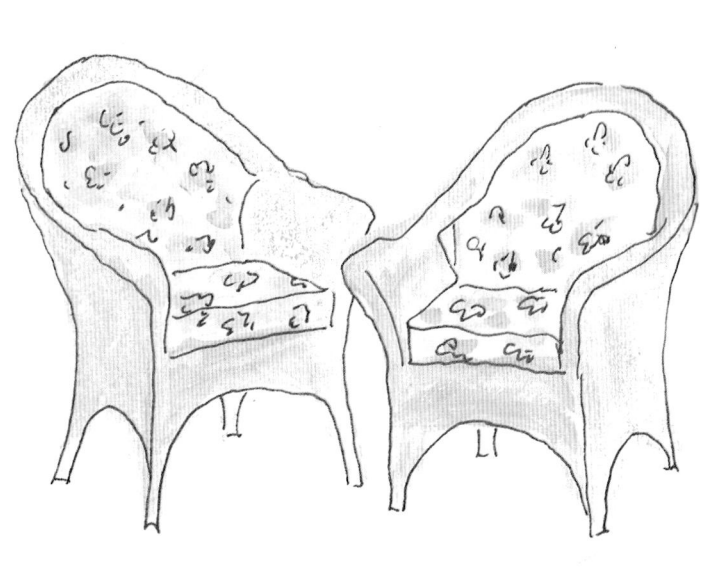

There
were
a thousand
things
my heart
forgot
to say.

◆   ◆   ◆

*Beautiful
memories
of
beautiful
times.*

Nothing
can
erase
them.

◆ ◆ ◆

There
are
no
endings,
only
beginnings.

◆ ◆ ◆

Remembering
is a
journey
our heart
takes
into a time
that was...

*...and
our
thoughts
are
the only
tickets
needed
to ride.*

◆ ◆ ◆

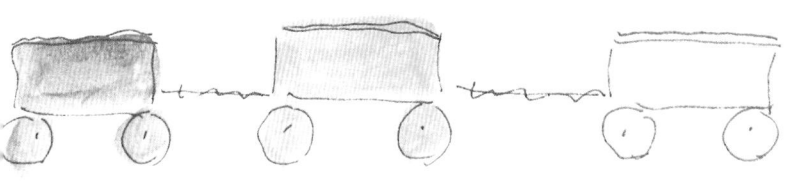

Do not
linger
too long
in
yesterday,
for
today
may hold
wonderful
surprises.

♦ ♦ ♦

Some people
bring
music
to those
whose
lives
they touch...

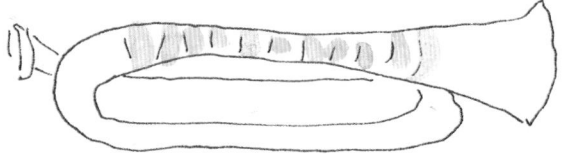

*...and
never know
the melody
lingers
on.*

♦ ♦ ♦

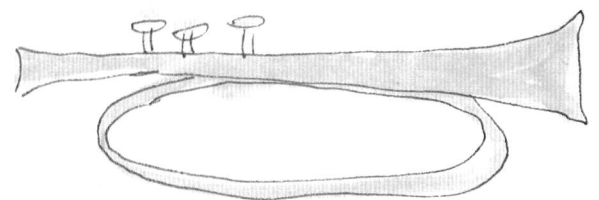

*Sweet
memories
are woven
from
the good
times.*

◆ ◆ ◆

I
think
of
you
still.

♦ ♦ ♦

Today
I saw
a child's
tin soldier
and
a loved-up
doll.

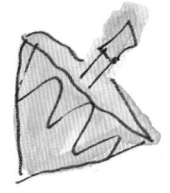

*I
thought
of
other places
and
other times
and
memories
we shared.*

◆ ◆ ◆

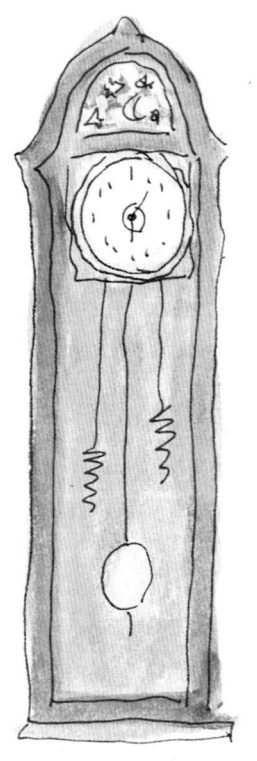

We
feel
sad...
but
we feel.

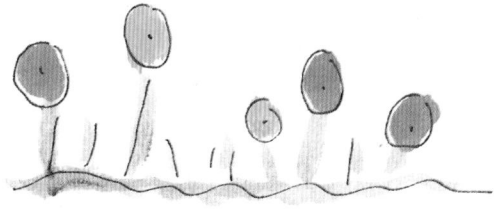

*Lucky
are
we.*

◆ ◆ ◆

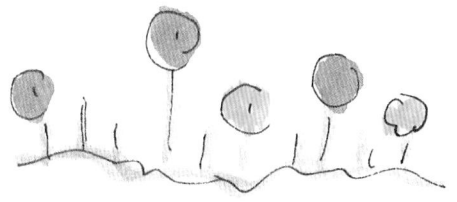

I
remember
a lot of
little
things
we shared
that made
me
happy.

◆ ◆ ◆

*All
the while...
did you know
we were
making
memories?*

◆ ◆ ◆

*It's
the sharing
of
ordinary
dreams…*

*...that
brings
the sweetest
memories
to mind.*

◆ ◆ ◆

We've
shared
too
much
to
forget.

♦ ♦ ♦

*Sometimes
our hearts
borrow
from
our
yesterdays.*

And
with each
remembrance
we meet
again
with those
we love.

◆　◆　◆

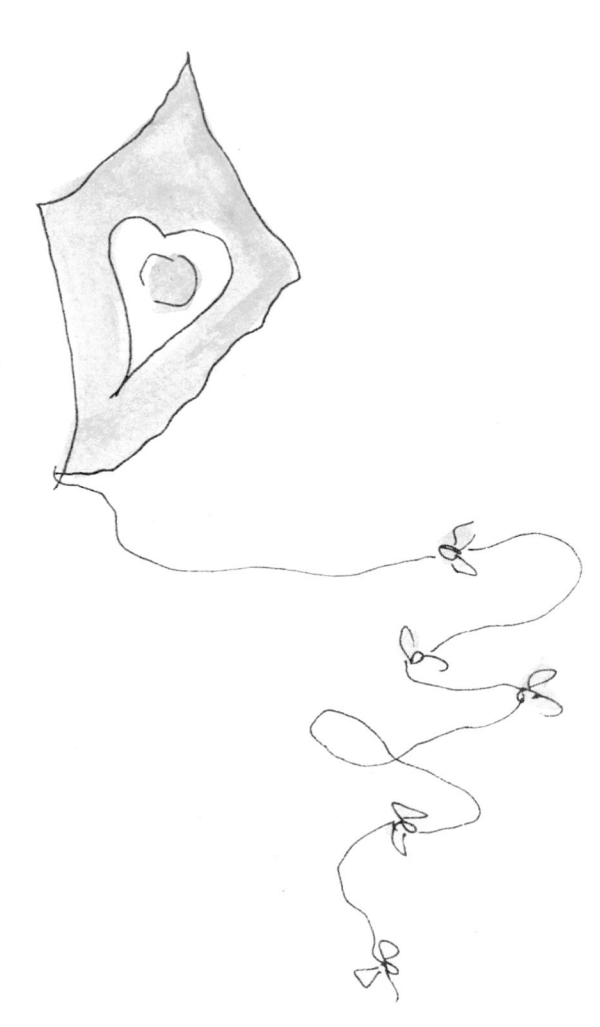

*We
need not
be
together
to share
a memory.
It
belongs
to both
of us.*

◆   ◆   ◆

*Some people
come into
our lives
and
quickly
go.*

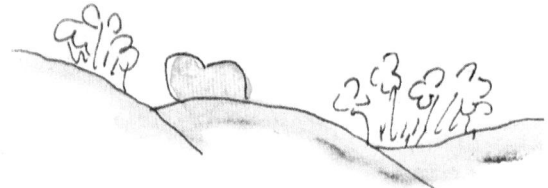

Some stay
for awhile,
leave footprints
on our hearts,
and we are
never, ever
the same.

◆ ◆ ◆

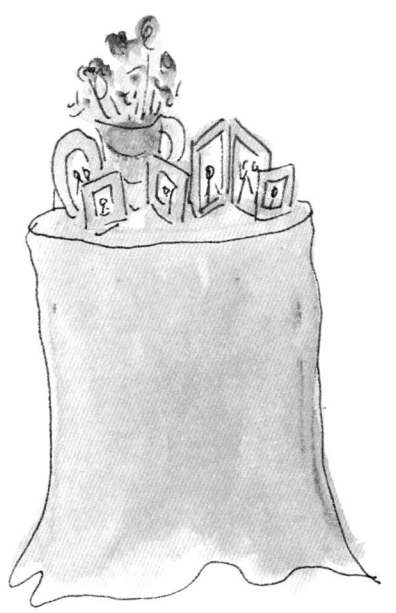

Those
whom
we have
loved
are with
us always,
for love
never dies.

◆ ◆ ◆

*Each
time
I look
at
something
I've loved...*

*...I realize
the difference
love makes
to our hearts,
and I
remember you.*

◆ ◆ ◆

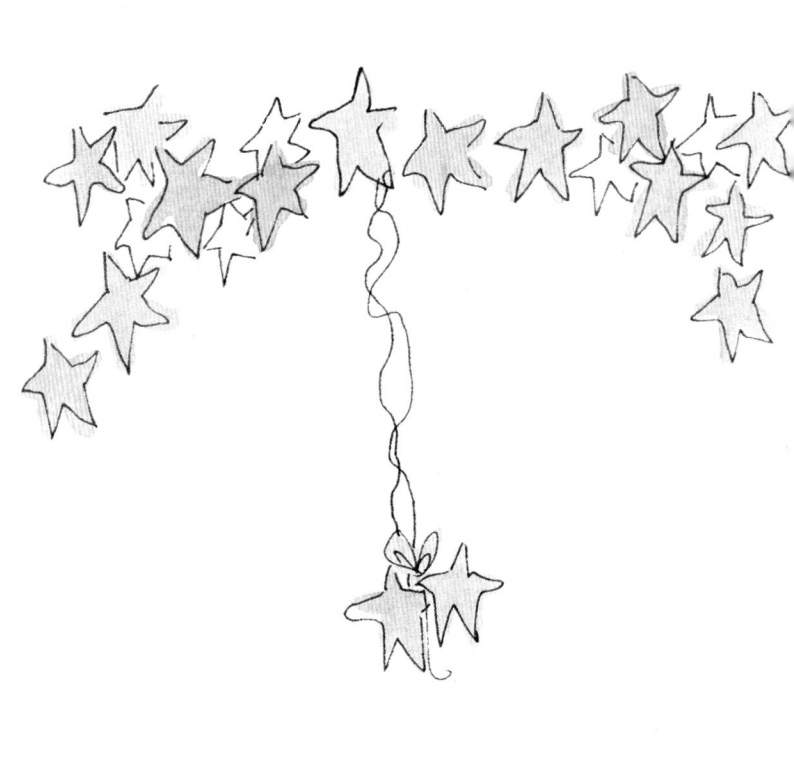

Perhaps
what we had
came from
a star,
and was
a kind of magic
only ours
to borrow.

♦ ♦ ♦

*When
I think
of you,
I silently
thank you
for
listening...*

*...and
for
always
being
my
friend.*

◆ ◆ ◆

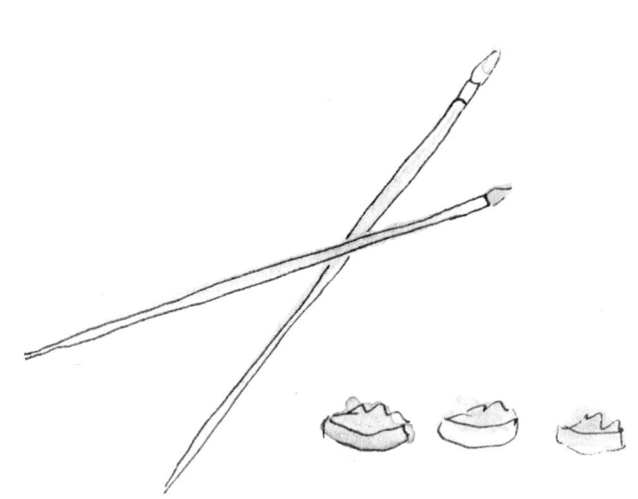

*Life
gives us
water-colored
memories
that last
forever.*

◆   ◆   ◆

*We
may
never
meet
again...*

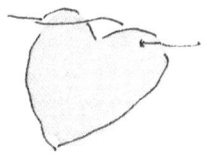

*...but
when we
remember,
we will be
close in heart.*

◆ ◆ ◆

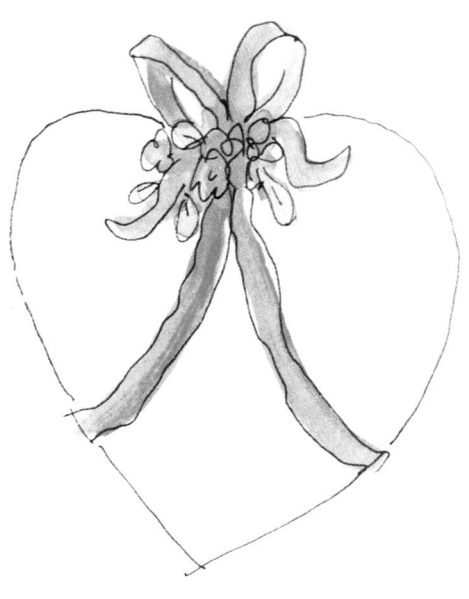

When
I close
my eyes
I can
touch
a favorite
dream,
and
I remember.

   ◆   ◆   ◆

*When
I'm alone
with my
thoughts,
I think
of all
the things...*

*...that
would have
never been...
...if you had
never been.*

♦ ♦ ♦

Our
memories
are wrapped
in ribbons
of the
heart.

◆   ◆   ◆

*When
I gather
memories
of ordinary days,
I remember...*

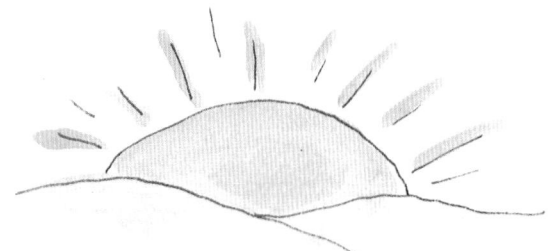

...how
special
you always
made them.

◆ ◆ ◆

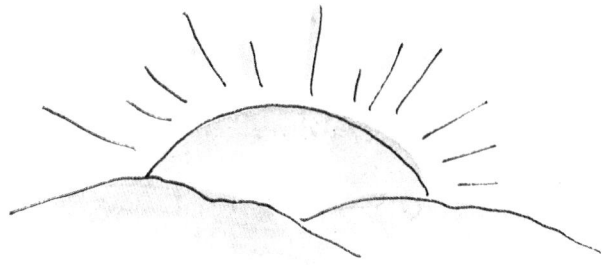

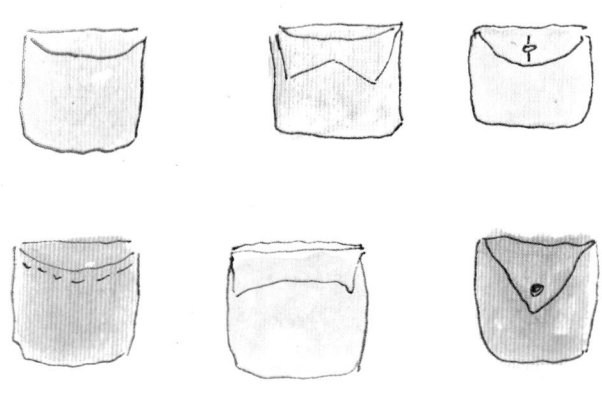

Thanks
for the
yesterdays
my heart
still holds
in its
pockets.

◆ ◆ ◆

*As people
come and go
in our lives,
each gives
something
to the
other...*

*...and
our lives
are
richer
for
having
touched.*

◆ ◆ ◆

I
find
traces
of
you
among
my souvenirs.

◆ ◆ ◆

*Although
our paths
may take
different
directions...*

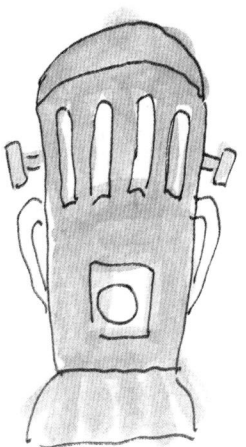

...you'll
always
be
a part
of
my life.

♦ ♦ ♦

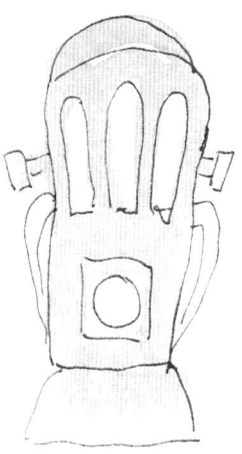

I find
bits and pieces
of you
my heart
has saved.

♦   ♦   ♦

*Sometimes
when
I'm alone,
something
will happen
to make
me
smile.*

I know
you, too,
would have been
touched
by the
moment,
and I
think
of you.

❖   ❖   ❖

*Thoughts
can take
us
anywhere.
Blessed
are we
who
remember.*

◆ ◆ ◆

*The
silent
tears
of the
heart
hurt
the
most.*

*There is
a time
to be
sad,
but
hearts
do
mend.*

♦ ♦ ♦

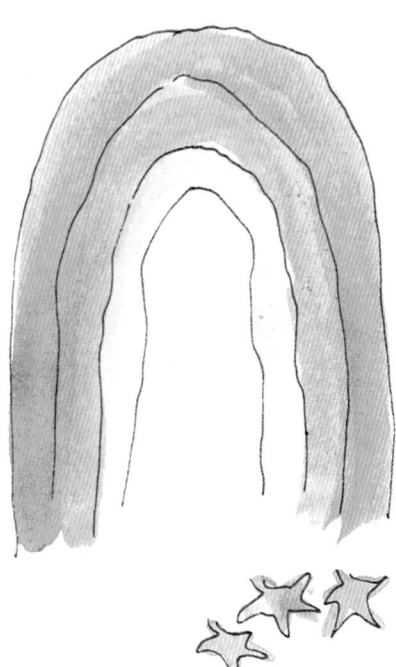

Beyond
the clouds,
behind
the rain,
there are
a thousand
rainbows.

◆ ◆ ◆

Sometimes
life
seems to
fall apart
a little
at a time.

*But
somehow,
some way,
it always
fits
together
again.*

♦ ♦ ♦

*Remember
it all,
and
be glad
for
the good
times.*

◆   ◆   ◆

The End

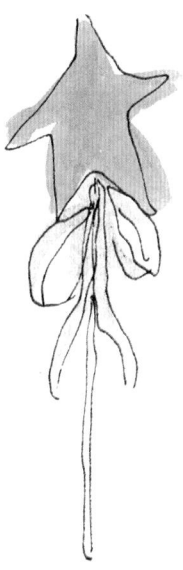

Flavia Weedn is a writer, painter and philosopher. Her life's work is about hope for the human spirit. "I want to reach people of all ages who've never been told, 'Wait a minute, look around you. It's wonderful to be alive and every one of us matters. We can all make a difference if we keep trying and never give up'". It is Flavia and her family's wish to awaken this spirit in each and every one of us. Flavia's messages are translated into many foreign languages, and are distributed worldwide.

For more information about Flavia or to receive the "Flavia Newsletter" write to:
Flavia
Box 42229 • Santa Barbara, CA 93140